Bits & Pieces
By Suzanne King Randall
Copyright 2012
All Rights Reserved
978-0-9858371-2-9

To my husband and sons for their tolerance
during this highly creative period.

Cover art: Suzanne King Randall

Bits & Pieces

The Mind Song

I wrote a song of sadness this morning; it filled me with so much sorrow, I had to change my tune. I will myself not to stay in such sadness. It would take me to the End of Days. I would collapse into the dust that blows in this Oklahoma wind. I would blow over the surface bringing sadness to an already sad world. So today, in spite of the wind and the aloneness I feel, I will change my song.

I'll write a little ditty that rhymes and won't let me go, or I'll write a song so sweet the day will flutter and land lightly on my heart. Which melody will fill my heart today, a happy tune to whistle and play along or a dirge in muddy waters?

I think I'll dance to someone else's tune and give my mind a rest. It thinks too much about too many problems; it builds a case for crazy. Stay out of that music hall. It sounds like an orchestra is tuning up, a cacophony of instruments. The bone walls don't keep it inside.

My mind has served so well so far I'd hate to misplace it now.

Suzanne King Randall

Greed is the root of all money.

Plastic is as plastic does.

T-shirts make a statement.

Welfare is: Not working.

This land has reservations.

Bits & Pieces

My Skin Remembers

My skin remembers—
your touch lingers, exploring,
loving fingers—my skin remembers—
My heart quickens—when it discovers my skin
remembers,
my heart quickens, exciting energy steps up the
pace—
rejoicing when I see your face, my heart quickens.
My mouth hungers, exchanging juices, tasting
you, my mouth hungers. soft breath, warm, moist,
laughter in your voice, My ears listen—
for your whisper of my name—
my ears listen—
and my eyes See,
soft brown eyes looking at me and my eyes see.
hands reaching out
fingers touching me—
and my skin remembers . . .

Suzanne King Randall

World peace depends on whose piece is whose.

Is there a moral minority?

Big Business is at the top of the food chain!

Condos are the capital defense.

Justice wears bifocals.

Bits & Pieces

Another One Bites the Dust

The city is screaming, crying out in pain,
an ambulance is racing down the street again.
Ripping time out of space,
advancing toward a field of grace . . .
—
Our souls are not used by life
awake and dream!
achieve the style of the soul . . . Imagination.
Welcome life into your space,
time will take care of the rest . . .

Suzanne King Randall

Save the Seals, we need them for Easter!

Do fruit flies become fairies?

In today's market, everyone loses interest.

The seat of justice has middle-aged spread.

A politician's worth never exceeds his abilities.

Bits & Pieces

Too Far

As I crunch along this well-worn path
I've severed all the bonds.
Reality says, "Too far, I've gone."
Too little yet remains,
too soon to find no one ever gains.

One Sip

I lick my lips slowly,
the taste of you remains
easily my tongue passes over . . . hot memories.
—
sensuous risings=taste buds

Suzanne King Randall

Children are remotely controlled.

Cowboys know how to Giddy up!

Now TV has captioned audiences!

Captioned audiences hear with their brains.

Wait till you get a clone of your own . . .

Bits & Pieces

Time and Time Again

And time will speak of many things,
it voices an opinion.
Its bell resounds the truth it rings . . . texture
woven lives interlocking . . .
threading through each other's time—
weaving precious moments into tapestry of a life,
colored with painterly strokes of time
we try to master every minute,
yes, time will tell . . . not you or I
invaluable time will tell, my love . . .
time is all and then it's gone.

Suzanne King Randall

Gorillas have long arms and tanks.

A 5-star general is a rank pretender.

Gray matter is all that matters!

Is genius a darker shade of gray?

Window cleaners hang out.

Bits & Pieces

And Time Again

Something broke in my heart last night.
I heard its sound in my throat.
"Loss," it cried. "Reality," I sighed.
Bits and pieces, scattered about
fragments of yesterday . . . pulling closer . . .
becoming whole . . . gathering soul.
Finding glimpses of tomorrow,
Something must die to make room for
what remains . . .

Suzanne King Randall

When leaves fall can trees be far behind?

Baseball players are often debased.

**We're not running out of time,
we're running away from it.**

Niagara falls or was it pushed?

Do stuffed shirts have vested interests?

Bits & Pieces

Mother, May I?

May I use the gifts you shared
may I take the dreams somewhere
may I cast away despair,
Mother, May I?

May I show myself to you?
Will you see and understand
evolutions of your fears
line the wrinkles of your hand.

Conversely, may I dispel all your fears
overcome these parts of you in me
Then I'm free to enjoy me
Mother, May I?

Stillborn ideas, dream positive dreams, again

Suzanne King Randall

Flies don't have air traffic controllers.

You can't come back until you get your hand stamped.

He who whispers is always heard.

A wife doesn't come along quietly.

Take another swing while you're still at bat.

Bits & Pieces

Only One Heart

Be quiet, heart—stop beating.
Everyone else can hear.
Enchantment, leave this heart of mine,
sing in another ear.
Love, be gone, leave me alone again,
your ache is tearing into my soul.
Release me . . . or
love me deeply, strongly with all the fire I have,
indulge my passions, hold me, for I will never be
the same . . .
I thought I was enough . . .

Suzanne King Randall

I give dust bunnies a good home!

Animals get their fur whole-sale!

Without crime, we could make prisons into condos!

The Middle East is such a Mesopotamia, it makes a Persian Gulf!

Is palimony a golden horse?

Bits & Pieces

Night Dress

Expectations too high—too much alone,
fill the nights with watery visions.
and of words, I shall not use for
anyone, but you, I shall make
poems and then blessed sleep.

Suzanne King Randall

Bring back the Pony Express!

Government spending for government waste!

Movers and shakers make waste.

Judges do it on the bench.

The radio makes listeners of us all.

Mirror, Mirror

Mirror images before my eyes,
reflecting back at any moment
take me back to my surprise,
delight my inner vision.
Frozen in a mirror, touching, discovering.
Suspended on a wall.
Feel the warmth of the moment.
The passage of time will never change
the Mirror. Smooth surface,
warm skin, cool glass, dim light
glowing from within,
emanating form the images.
The performance is sublime.
The players know the taste of excellence.
The truth is in the mirror.

Suzanne King Randall

Luxury stimulates the economy.

Lawyers wear briefs.

Police pick up, but do they deliver?

Self-first preservation!

Hypocrites know the truth
and choose not to tell it.

Drinking Water

Sweet gentle laps the water makes,
hypnotic in the summer sun.
Feel the closeness in the air, the
closeness wrapped around our bodies,
sticky with heat,
taste it,
lap it,
like the water laps the earth into it . . .

Last Laugh

To last without
is hard at best,
It's best to last at all.
Too soon we last
to best at least,
Lest last laugh
we recall.

Suzanne King Randall

Clones take a likin' to you.

The ego is a short trip.

AWACS are Tinker Toys!

The Army does an about face.

You can't keep a good plane down.

Bits & Pieces

Indian Giver

Shine proudly, silent in your world
running the tapes for others—recording
new memories for yourself.
Achieving the light of the lime—
no special meaning of time—
sexual pleasures, sublime.
It's all a matter of time.

Warmth, comfort, softness—
permission to give and to take—
nurturing so dear.
Responding so clear
makes even a stubborn heart break.

Giving is a special gift unto itself,
the discovery of which will never mean
as much as it does at this moment.
In order to have this gift you must be able
to recognize it in others.
It's fanning a fire, it's
breathing desire and exposure of
vulnerable hearts.

Suzanne King Randall

Do Texans have ten gallon heads?

Cowboys know where to step.

**If we all ran toward the East,
would the Earth spin faster?**

Commuting is a cattle drive.

**Our rivers are so full of waste,
they drag themselves to the shore.**

Heart Smiles

In my dreams—I'm full, complete.
My heart smiles, warms my eyes,
when I look into your face.
Behind your eyes I see your heart smiles.
I stretch, catlike on satin pillows,
waiting, luxuriating, relishing,
my heart laughs out loud—
The anticipation, the lust, the ecstasy,
I feel your heart laughing, too.
We share the same soul, too short a time,
in my dreams,
but then,
when our eyes greet across a room,
our hearts smile . . .

Suzanne King Randall

I'll have ham and cheese,
and hold the preservatives!

If we are what we eat,
we should be well preserved!

May the Air Force be with you.

Sergeants have three stripes against them.

The Air Force is breaking wind.

Bits & Pieces

Mental Stroke

Envisioned in my head, a cinema of shapes,
bright living color—
soothing blacks and softest grays.
Reach-out Red, Screaming Eagle Yellow,
jumping for attention, only to be limited
by a canvas and by me.
Such releases vibrate in my thought patterns,
squelch my verbal responses,
demand to show themselves.
The color must have a place to live.
I give it that, but can't I keep the moments sublime
and the experiences personal treasures before the
invasion of another human eye?

Suzanne King Randall

Crows have crow's feet, too.

Women are super-chargers!

Life is great at 45.
You get a change whether
you need one or not!

Beware of clap-traps!

I love fast cars and slow men.

Bits & Pieces

At Random

Reality covers my body with wrinkles,
causes my emotions to scatter,
fills my brain with ideas
that try so hard to matter . . .

Drawing myself up, getting a hold, a grip
passing through a doorway,
careful not to slip.

I felt old again last night.
Everyone must feel this fright.
With candles burning into the night,
I felt the fear of age last night . . .

The rhythm still beats in my youthful heart,
the call is unmistakable.
The quiet is an awakening thought . . .
My love of life unshakable . . .

Suzanne King Randall

Satan is a horny devil!

Night sounds are darker than day sounds.

Desegregated minorities.

Pearls are little irritations.

Bigots feed on mal-contents!

Bits & Pieces

Out On The River Bottom

Two places at once . . .
Back to the earth, down on the ground
feeling the beat, just south of town.
Two bodies rising out under the stars,
feeling the beat, sailing to Mars.
Lusting in life, night all around
feeling the beat, pounding the ground . . .

Unlearn

Trying . . . rooting around , kicking debris
away from my nest. I am where I am
touching some lives, making a distance.
Coming out of the dark.
Taking the path of least resistance.

Suzanne King Randall

Don't let America go to pot!

Knowledge is the root of all wisdom.

Psychologists heal my "self."

When He answers, don't hang up!

Incarceration can be hazardous to your health.

Bits & Pieces

Dealing

Rounding the corner, knowing, feeling,
dealing with life.
Loving the living, living the strife.
Rounding the corner, turning the key,
follow the path that leads you to me.
Reach for a flower, a smile and the sun,
feel the warm breeze
when this day is done.
Enjoy all my songs, sing-a-long if you feel,
trust my energy,
Know that I'm real . . .

Suzanne King Randall

The electric chair is the seat of justice.

Near-sighted people are short sighted.

I'll give it a 95, I like the beat.

Gray power is the last word.

Super-natural is unnatural.

Bits & Pieces

Navy Blue

My thoughts of you are navy blue
as mellow as the night.
They fold around me like the dew
and await your warming light.

I hear your slightest whisper.
my heart quickens in response
to all you are inviting—I must
stop to take a chance.

Navy blue silk that whispers
softly, as it slips and falls away,
revealing inner secrets of the hopes of yesterday.

Suzanne King Randall

Indians have Great Spirit!

Here lies a man of truth.

Charity begins at home . . .

**Your number could be up
before you get it memorized.**

**Memories must be relived
to make them better.**

Bits & Pieces

No Speed Limit

Speeding through light
exposing thought to scrutiny
only the strongest survive
The Bare Bulb . . .

Rock of Ages

Full of hope . . . is that a prayer?
A glimpse of religion there?
tried and true separate view
only when you follow through.

Stepping on the smoothest stones,
I keep my balance.

Suzanne King Randall

Insane asylums are houses of ill repute!

Nurses shot-put.

Sickle cell anemia is a grim reaper.

Funny farms are not funny.

EKG is a ticker tape.

Bits & Pieces

Uncovered Bed

Visages of warm soft flesh
invitations in the eyes—
intimacies in whispers—
murmured laughter, murmured sighs
secrets shared, and yet, untold—
silken sheets, together bold.

Time Capsule

Time is a glistening jewel, precious—illusive.
Time is now, valued until the end of—
Kind to some, hurtful to others—
When it's used well, it is all there is.

Suzanne King Randall

Graciousness can't be bought.

How many people have had it today?

Alimony is a discouraging word.

Working mothers have hard hats!

**Men have only one thing
on their mind, at a time.**

Bits & Pieces

Just Passing Through

Hot wind parches summer flowers,
peels layers away from the earth—
exposes,
I feel its breath burn moments in time.

As I scoop up warm grains of sand,
I smile at the sunset—
knowing, we'll come this way again.

Pioneer Woman

Pioneer spirit, individual free in her own skin
full of beauty, fully bloomed within.
Traveling, making her own foot prints,
inward to oneness.

I'll be your champion
you'll be mine.

Suzanne King Randall

Life of man is ages long.

The Age of Reason is 30 or older.

Late bloomers are the last to grow.

I'm just peddling my life cycle as fast as I can.

Four eyes are better than none.

Bits & Pieces

Behind My Eyes

I touch your face—so gently—
I feel your softness in my mouth
I smell your hair, your warmth, I taste you
I do all this—when you're about.

I run my tongue across smooth skin,
I circle your nipples—watch them rise—
kiss you up and down your thighs.
I do all this—behind my eyes.

and then—we finally are together.
I feel energy in every pore, as
I hold you ever closer,
my heart pounds me to the core.
I do all this and ask for more . . .

I always knew I would come this way, but
yesterday, I did not know it would be today..

Suzanne King Randall

Silence is louder than words.

Music puts a song in your heart.

There's no end to a good beginning.

The way to a man's heart is a triple bypass.

Perpetual motion is a driving force.

Another Time

Life is a matter of timing, act, react—timing
Passivity, activity
involvement, later—
Kiss and tell, or not—
get closer to it
embrace it—
It's just a matter of time . . .

Deco

Hot breath against cool glass—
a raindrop or a tear?
Paper dreams crumpled in a corner,
tossed in collected debris.
Ragged edges, aged and yellowed
thoughts bent back upon themselves.
Imagination never fails,
riding on such paper trails.

Suzanne King Randall

Don't tell everything you know,
even if it doesn't take very long.

Sun City is the last resort.

The Ice Age is about 37.

Crow's feet come in pairs.

Life is a laugh-long joke.

Bits & Pieces

Whoops!

Oh, whoops! I hit the skids.
I slammed into a wall;
an expectation wasn't met,
I had to sit and bawl.
My days had all been full of fun,
my nights were less, but bearable . . .
so then that expectation grew,
anticipation's terrible.

Ebbing

Putting on the night like a sleek satin gown,
I feel the pills sway my thoughts
around like a breeze.
Warm, comforting water engulfs me
as I slide away to the sea.

Suzanne King Randall

Rumpled-Still-Skin.

A forgetful man is best forgotten.

Schizophrenia is two-faced.

A schizophrenic can double-talk.

A clone can be beside himself!

Bits & Pieces

Winter Wood

Vermillion cast across heavy pelts—
crunch of snow, advancing sound—
Hot breath in frozen air—
Heart beats pound ancient memories
quiet cold creeping down.
THE WOLF IS AT THE DOOR . . .

Bird On a Wire

Perched carefully on top my bicycle.
The 10 foot pole in my sweating hands dips
slowly toward the left.
The cable below my pedals begins to sway.
I pause to look down,
downward to the sawdust floor.
I notice with a great burst of adrenaline,
I'M WORKING WITHOUT A NET !!!

Suzanne King Randall

Keep computers at arm's length.

I'm on my third wish!

It's hard to peddle your wares when they keep getting caught in your spokes.

Some people pretend to be people.

An old saying is a voice from the past.

Bits & Pieces

Heart Talk

My head is pounding— What's the rush?
My heart is saying it's a crush—
the thoughts we've shared, once
made me blush—

Tender words, cling ever near
protect and nourish without fear—
response is easy with a mind,
But with a heart be extra kind
—
Imaginings are reflections cast,
illusive visions of the past.

Suzanne King Randall

Optimism is buying a one-way ticket.

High school students are anti-semantics!

How do you spell Polish?

Do blank minds create blank verse?

Without class, we would all be illiterate!

I, Sea

Watching the seagulls lay into a thermal gust
relaxed, at peace,
constant pounding of the waves—
sweet sticky air forecasting a storm,
we take our footprints so seriously . . .

Suzanne King Randall

A college demonstration is a show and tell.

Med school is Greek to me.

A Greek Myth could be a Roman Madam.

America is too young to quote.

Greased palms are dirty.

Bits & Pieces

My Word

Many words and syllables pass through the atmosphere.
Thoughts expressed cling to those,
aware enough to hear . . .
—
Lust puts love in motion.

Autumn

Indian summer evolves slowly
inhaling heat for winter fuel,
perspiring impurities, exhaling colors.
It warms our hibernating sleep.

Suzanne King Randall

Everyman casts the same shadow.

Oil quiets a squeaky wheel.

The odds are never even.

Can consumers get consumption?

Clock watching is time consuming.

Bits & Pieces

I Watched

I watched your strength diminish—
your body trembled as your spirit slipped away.
My love for you exploded in my heart.
Each particle of love as fine as stardust,
as heavy as emotion—timeless.

Wherever I find your spirit,
in whatever form,
I will acknowledge your presence . . .

Suzanne King Randall

Shuffling is out, prancing is in.

The criminal mind is a cell block long.

Crowned heads never recover.

Republicans never forget.

Re-United States.

Bits & Pieces

Heads Up!

My life has been so full, so rich,
I feel its power surge within.
Power emanating from my history, my past,
keeps my head up proudly.
Now I know just where I stand—
a head above the rest . . .

Suzanne King Randall

Bring back Leprechauns.

Hereditary factors are in the jeans.

If you have IT, don't sell IT.

If you like IT have IT bronzed.

When you're indentured, does that mean you're a slave to the dentist?

Bits & Pieces

Night Birds

Night birds closing wings around shadows
heated by day—
long discussions remain in the air
fevered wishes hammer home—
Neon statements pushing light—
intrusions—
moonlight washes the day away—
evolution—
gentle sounds of morning—
Awakenings . . .

Suzanne King Randall

There are Wise and Otherwise!

Decisions are the hardest things to make.

We all speak in foreign tongues.

Arabs have oily hands.

When buck passer speaks, no one listens.

Bits & Pieces

On Call

Explain—
tell me
Help me to know— What is the meaning?
Why the glow?
It starts far down deep inside—
building from my depths below!

Your voice, your name, your call
brings up this warmth
you could be anybody—
you're not of course—

you bring my senses up, heightened,
make my attention peak—
before you even speak—
So long I've been alone—
so long I've felt misunderstood—
so long in happening—
I wondered if it ever would.

I wonder if I should pay attention to you at all?
And then you start it all again—You call . . .

Suzanne King Randall

Bad taste lingers on.

Down with duck-billed platitudes.

Thoroughbreds wear purses.

Dogs are four steps ahead of you.

Left fielders catch flies.

Bits & Pieces

It's Twelve O'clock

From the deep recesses of the house
the gentle "bong" of the clock
brought my thoughts to my childhood.
The peacefulness of the atmosphere
felt like deep breathing—
Bong—it's peaceful here
Bong—the clock chime sounds—
Bong—it's tone is clear—and round—
Bong—the time has passed so fast—
Bong—the tempo breathes the time away—
Bong—like my heartbeat when love is near—
Bong—repeating still another day—
Bong—the beats come and go—never stay—
Bong—My life feels like a new beginning.
Bong—its time to pay attention to my self.
Bong—feel the peace I have within me.
Bong—and put my past high on a shelf . . .
It's twelve o'clock..

Reality is illusion—
playing out a life of its own.
Ideas presume knowledge.

Suzanne King Randall

Democracy is a two-party line.

Uncle Sam is You.

Memories are made right here.

What's the worst that can happen?

Gum keeps your teeth in.

Bits & Pieces

Lucky Star

Tonight is just another night
casting away the light,
sending it to the other side.
Abandoning reality,
the night whispers fantasies in my ear.
How fortunate you are, lucky star.

Suzanne King Randall

The human race is a tie!

Random work for random people.

The bowels of the earth are the waste of time!

Governments are run with tricks and treaties.

Loss of memories is a circuit breaker.

Bits & Pieces

Babel, the Tower of

Cacophony of voices—Babel, the Tower of
loose colors of weavings
Too many dialects to make a song
too many songs to make a language.
What is this society?
Too Many?
Too many voices make a word—
never heard, never heard,

a climb too high—
a murmur low.
Retreating, too far below.
Vocabulary needs a dictionary.
Remembering is a plus:
Babel, The Tower of
infusions— living dust.
The voices will be buried, laughing,
when the crust is hardening..
Babel, The Tower of.

Suzanne King Randall

Ages go.

**The last of the Red Hot Mamas
is an Old Mother.**

Birth control is a growing business.

Martyrs won't do it at all.

**A wise man speaks slowly
so the rest can understand.**

Bits & Pieces

Going Through a Change Whether You Need It or Not

Gradual changes—subtle all the while, changes
unnoticed when they happen—
unrecorded in their infinitesimal beginning.
becoming, evolving,
reality—a fact.
The truth is in the pudding—
My mirror's looking back.

Beyond the great divide
when we jump over the crack—
remembered uneven beginnings—
The future erases past tracks . . .

Suzanne King Randall

Fairies fly and never land.

The male is the staff of life,
but the female is the carrier.

Grass has a mind of its own.

Most everything is in plane view.

Rich people hire it done.

Bits & Pieces

Of Strength

My Grandpa's voice recalls me—his voice
deep and rich.
Narrating imaginings, acting all the parts
telling stories in the dark—
There's comfort in the recall—

There's loss in the comfort—
and there's strength in the loss—
Strength narrates sensitivity—
in a warm dry place (I see his face).

Belonging—responding to the memories—
My Grandma's words from other rooms
that no longer exist—

the quiet nature of her soul is with me still—
the patterns of her fabric threading through my
veins—

irony remains.

Suzanne King Randall

The strong shall inherit the weak.

The faster you run,
the more rain drops you hit.

Booze finds its own level.

Rolling stones gather speed.

Congress has too many bills to pay now!

Bits & Pieces

Hug

Wrapped in my own arms
I feel my Mother's warmth—
I tighten my hug as often she did
and rocked me—back and forth.

It's not tight enough or long enough, but
there is a strength in knowing
that she once did and she would again,
if she only could . . . I know she always would . . .
Love Me.

Suzanne King Randall

Oh, Columbia, the gem of the cosmos!

The Evil Eye never blinks.

Congress makes issues out of everything.

Las Vegas is full of crap shooters.

Drunk driving is an arrested development.

Bits & Pieces

Watch My Dust

Blur the sights lit by the sun
and another day is done—
I breathe, the earth sighs in the wind—
I eat, the dead replenish my body—
I laugh, the sun warms my skin—
I cry, the rain falls and drowns the pain—
lying in my buried soul, forcing it to the surface—
airing it in my breath—the warm breeze.
I love and color runs through my heart
with spring the years pass
I am dust . . .

Tread lightly on my dust . . . you will be me one
day . . .

Suzanne King Randall

After your first mistake, the rest become easier.

**Forced retirement is a waste
of natural resources.**

The road to success is a toll road.

Gifted people send out.

Overachievers overdo it.

Bits & Pieces

Rock A Bye

My cradle was full of my Mother's dreams
The bough carried songs to my heart
Time rocks-a-way on the words
and I still hear what I heard.

Suzanne King Randall

The Universe is a one-sided conversation.

Football fans are athletic supporters.

Baseball is catching.

The mystery for today is: What's in our meat?

A crow bar is for singles.

Bits & Pieces

Mist

Mist whispers of time
crossing destinies, vapors of lives,
replenishing in our faces
filling the space as we create—ourselves.

lasting long past desire,
touching everything
relating to every living thing,
We still lack the confidence to care . . .

Suzanne King Randall

Some women have beauty an inch thick.

Labels are the signs of the times.

Hitchhikers get carried away.

Old Indians are braver.

America, the home of the free and the Braves.

Bits & Pieces

Leave Running

Mysterious looming darkness—
warm black, telling nothing, saying all—
Masquerading as human, the burial ground
dots the hillside, alerting my senses . . .

Nothing changes until it does
No one ever sees it until they do,
The Physics of Perception

Pavement races under my feet, yet I'm still.
fantasies paint motion pictures in my mind.
Calling out, craving,
Did I dream you?

Was that a long euphoric dream state I was in?
tossing and turning down emotional roads .
Sweet dreams,
Leave running.

Suzanne King Randall

So, material things are immaterial.

Celebrate the bad times;
there are more of them.

Beaches are full of the sands of time.

Dogs are people, too.

Executive toys are city blocks.

Bits & Pieces

Way Beyond

Beyond the crowds
beyond the streets,
the voices of the past
entreat—

Like a siren calling
home all the ages
come and gone—

While I sit in contemplation,
the voices speak in expectation . . .
Wonder in the dust
way beyond.

Suzanne King Randall

Don't collect nuts or bar flies.

Glasses are a pane.

Frowns are frowned upon.

Predestination or post-destination?

Liars know the truth and try to hide it.

Bits & Pieces

Train of Thought

Metal grazing metal
Scrunching a rhythm
through the quilted landscape.

Transparent veils of time
Peal away forbidden thoughts
evolution changes reality's complexion.

Politics

Reaching with aching muscles
stretching thoughts to match deeds
trying very hard to please . . .
Kissing someone's ass is a disease . . . .

Suzanne King Randall

There are two sides to every border.

Politicians speak double-talk fluently.

Are Civil Wars fought be civilians?

The peace dove is a bird of pray.

We are life in the Universe!

Bits & Pieces

Observation

My face cracked
and the mirror didn't.
Another lesson to be learned.
Obviously an oversight.
For surely the mirror should have.
The mirror sees all,
tells all,
And still can keep a straight face.

Who is it?

I'm on fire, pray for rain . . .
Inspired by thought,
The beast turns pale
behind the veil of humanness—

—

Evolution doth make monkeys of us all.

Suzanne King Randall

Why not teach; no one else does.

Teachers spread the word.

Math teachers are calculating!

English is just another spoken word.

History is a thing of the past.

Mankind

I saw your face, Mankind. It understood.
You held my hand, led me and it was good.
The knowing look deep in brown eyes,
Mankind sees and Mankind sighs.

You gently cupped me in your hands
Thank you for being one Kind Man.

Suzanne King Randall

Teachers do it everywhere.

Keep our seas shining.

Labor is a big pain.

Conception of time is clockwise.

Things beget things.

Bits & Pieces

The Big, Bad Wolf

Loneliness makes the night a darker black,
it creeps through the cracks, past outer barriers,
chilling my emotions to a frozen paralysis.
It reminds me of my mortality!!!

Aloneness can do that . . . some nights.

Suzanne King Randall

There are more things than people.

A smile defies the law of gravity.

Secretaries are prestidigitators.

Oil wells are dip sticks.

Stand up and be counted;
just don't become a number.

Bits & Pieces

In Parting

I have drunk from your well, beloved.
My heart has been nourished by your heart—
My life has been enhanced by your presence.
My step is stronger for having walked with you.
My skin will always remember,
I can taste you still . . .

Suzanne King Randall

Construction workers get plastered.

A painting is a pigment of your imagination.

A step is a foot long.

Some people relate to animation.

Everybody comes out of the closet sometime!

Bits & Pieces

Bright Idea

Incandescent energy warms harsh images.
Night slows day's pace.
In the shadows, dreams replay the day.
Shadows deepen to the dark side
surrounding my thoughts
with comforting cool arms.
The parameter of light protects who's in it . . .

Suzanne King Randall

When you're rich and famous,
what else is new?

Cheese is a certain smile.

Obstacles grow from seeds of doubt.

Trains leave big tracks.

Retain the trains!

www.ingramcontent.com/pod-product-compliance
Lightning Source LLC
Chambersburg PA
CBHW071723040426
42446CB00011B/2198